This planner belongs to::

Also by Sze Wing Vetault:

Books

Goddess with Many Faces

21 Days of Inspiration

For more information, please visit:
www.SzeWingVetault.com

This Goddess Planner is created by Sze Wing Vetault
Copyright © 2020 by Sze Wing Vetault. All rights reserved.

How to Use This Planner

Thank you so much for embarking on your goddess journey with me!

This goddess planner is more than just a tool to plan your year ahead. It is a companion that will help you manifest your deepest desires with clarity and heart. In this planner, you will find journaling pages to record your new moon intentions and full moon releases each month. At the end of the planner, you will also find a Year-End Review and New Year Wish List for you to celebrate the year and dream ahead for the next.

A part of uncovering your feminine wisdom is being able to follow your energy ebb and flow. There are some days in a month where you may feel more creative, productive or energetic. On the other hand, there are times you may need extra rest or a quiet time to reflect. Ideas sprout when we allow time and space for our minds to empty. That's why I have created the weekly check-in and weekly planner pages with the moon and menstrual cycle in mind. If for any reasons you are not menstruating, you can follow the moon cycle to that effect.

This planner is designed to help you plan your work, play and rest more effectively. By regularly using the planner, you will naturally become more aware of your body's rhythms and emotional needs.

I am a firm believer in the benefits of spiritual practices such as meditation, yoga, prayer as well as evidence-based good habits. They can work wonderfully together to improve our overall well-being. The Weekly To-Do list, Universe To-Do list and Habit Tracker are included for that reason. There is no right or wrong way of using this planner. Use what you need, try and explore what works best for you. I hope you enjoy this planner and it grows with you in this coming year.

With love,

Sze Wing Vétault

12-Months Plan

What are your dreams?
Write down your new wishes/goals/dreams below:

The Moon Cycle

 **New Moon:** It's time to make a fresh start, set new intentions, sow new seeds, initiate new projects. Just keep it easy and light while the energy is still new.

 **Waxing Moon:** The moon is growing larger, energy is rising and expanding. It's a good time for brainstorming, planning and taking actions. Perfect for creating momentum or trying something new.

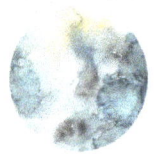 **Full Moon:** The moon is full in the sky, energy is peaking and it's time to be seen or heard. Great time to make an announcement, launch or pitch a project/product and connect or celebrate with others.

 **Waning Moon:** The moon is growing smaller in the sky. Energy is reducing and signaling a time to finish up loose ends and complete the work you have in hand.

 **Balsamic Moon:** "Balsamic" means healing and soothing. As the moon continues to grow smaller, it's time to make peace with where you are and appreciate all the blessings in your life. Trust in divine timing.

 **Dark Moon:** This is the day before new moon begins. It's a good time to rest and reflect. You may feel you need a bath or go to bed early. Slow down and relax.

The Menstrual Cycle

Menstrual Phase (Day 1-5)
- It begins on the first day of a woman's menstrual cycle
- Corresponds to the New Moon Phase
- Self-care ideas: Take a bath or a nap, meditate, journal or read. Use essential oils to relax. Don't overschedule and make space in your calendar.

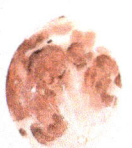
Follicular Phase (Day 6-13)
- Oestrogen level starts to rise, feel-good brain chemicals increase
- Corresponds to the Waxing Moon Phase
- Self-care ideas: Start a new project, try a new workout, initiate a girls-day/night-out, be brave and go for an adventure!

Ovulation Phase (Day 14-16)
- The most fertile time of a woman's cycle.
- Corresponds to the Full Moon Phase
- Self-care ideas: Go for a date-night, social gathering, networking, reach out to people.

Luteal Phase (Day 17-28)
- After releasing the egg, the progesterone level rises and mood changes
- Corresponds to the Waning Moon Phase
- Self-care ideas: declutter, tidy up, finish up projects, analyse what happened, go for 1-1 time with a friend, meditate.

*This guide shows a 28-day cycle. Some women's cycle may be longer or shorter.

M	T	W	T	F	S	S

Turning It Over

My To-Do List   **Universe To-Do List**

New Moon Intentions

Full Moon Release

My Weekly Planner

DATE:

MOON PHASE: NEW MOON / WAXING / FULL MOON / WANING

FOCUS: REST. REFLECT. SET INTENTION / PLAN. INITIATE. ACTION
CONNECT. BE SEEN. RELEASE / COMPLETE. DELIVER. LET GO

TOP 3 PRIORITIES: **REMINDER:**

TO-DO LIST:

Weekly Schedule

Appointments / Workout / Meals

Date:

Monday

Tuesday

Wednesday

Thursday

Friday

Saturday

Sunday

Note

Weekly Check-In

DATE:

MOON PHASE:

CYCLE: Menstrual / Follicular / Ovulation / Luteal

MOOD:

BODY
How's your energy this week?

MIND
What is on your mind?

SPIRIT
How are you feeling?

Ideas for self-care practices:

Habit Tracker

KEY FOCUS FOR THIS WEEK:

MY GOOD HABITS | M | T | W | TH | F | S | S

_____ ○ ○ ○ ○ ○ ○ ○

_____ ○ ○ ○ ○ ○ ○ ○

_____ ○ ○ ○ ○ ○ ○ ○

_____ ○ ○ ○ ○ ○ ○ ○

_____ ○ ○ ○ ○ ○ ○ ○

_____ ○ ○ ○ ○ ○ ○ ○

_____ ○ ○ ○ ○ ○ ○ ○

_____ ○ ○ ○ ○ ○ ○ ○

NOTE:

My Weekly Planner

DATE:

MOON PHASE: NEW MOON / WAXING / FULL MOON / WANING

FOCUS: REST. REFLECT. SET INTENTION / PLAN. INITIATE. ACTION
CONNECT. BE SEEN. RELEASE / COMPLETE. DELIVER. LET GO

TOP 3 PRIORITIES: **REMINDER:**

TO-DO LIST:

Weekly Schedule

Appointments / Workout / Meals

Date:

Monday

Tuesday

Wednesday

Thursday

Friday

Saturday

Sunday

Note

Weekly Check-In

DATE:

MOON PHASE:

CYCLE: Menstrual / Follicular / Ovulation / Luteal

MOOD:

BODY
How's your energy this week?

MIND
What is on your mind?

SPIRIT
How are you feeling?

Ideas for self-care practices:

Habit Tracker

KEY FOCUS FOR THIS WEEK:

MY GOOD HABITS   M   T   W   TH   F   S   S

_____ ○ ○ ○ ○ ○ ○ ○

_____ ○ ○ ○ ○ ○ ○ ○

_____ ○ ○ ○ ○ ○ ○ ○

_____ ○ ○ ○ ○ ○ ○ ○

_____ ○ ○ ○ ○ ○ ○ ○

_____ ○ ○ ○ ○ ○ ○ ○

_____ ○ ○ ○ ○ ○ ○ ○

_____ ○ ○ ○ ○ ○ ○ ○

NOTE:

My Weekly Planner

DATE:

MOON PHASE: NEW MOON / WAXING / FULL MOON / WANING

FOCUS: REST. REFLECT. SET INTENTION / PLAN. INITIATE. ACTION
CONNECT. BE SEEN. RELEASE / COMPLETE. DELIVER. LET GO

TOP 3 PRIORITIES: **REMINDER:**

TO-DO LIST:

Weekly Schedule
Appointments / Workout / Meals

Date:

Monday

Tuesday

Wednesday

Thursday

Friday

Saturday

Sunday

Note

Weekly Check-In

DATE:

MOON PHASE:

CYCLE: Menstrual / Follicular / Ovulation / Luteal

MOOD:

BODY
How's your energy this week?

MIND
What is on your mind?

SPIRIT
How are you feeling?

Ideas for self-care practices:

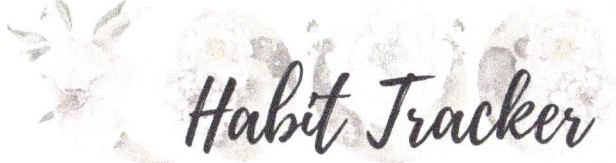

Habit Tracker

KEY FOCUS FOR THIS WEEK:

MY GOOD HABITS   M   T   W   TH   F   S   S

_____

_____

_____

_____

_____

_____

_____

_____

NOTE:

My Weekly Planner

DATE:

MOON PHASE: NEW MOON / WAXING / FULL MOON / WANING

FOCUS: REST. REFLECT. SET INTENTION / PLAN. INITIATE. ACTION
CONNECT. BE SEEN. RELEASE / COMPLETE. DELIVER. LET GO

TOP 3 PRIORITIES: **REMINDER:**

TO-DO LIST:

Weekly Schedule

Appointments / Workout / Meals

Date:

Monday

Tuesday

Wednesday

Thursday

Friday

Saturday

Sunday

Note

Weekly Check-In

DATE:

MOON PHASE:

CYCLE: Menstrual / Follicular / Ovulation / Luteal

MOOD:

BODY
How's your energy this week?

MIND
What is on your mind?

SPIRIT
How are you feeling?

Ideas for self-care practices:

Habit Tracker

KEY FOCUS FOR THIS WEEK:

MY GOOD HABITS   M   T   W   TH   F   S   S

_____ ○ ○ ○ ○ ○ ○ ○

_____ ○ ○ ○ ○ ○ ○ ○

_____ ○ ○ ○ ○ ○ ○ ○

_____ ○ ○ ○ ○ ○ ○ ○

_____ ○ ○ ○ ○ ○ ○ ○

_____ ○ ○ ○ ○ ○ ○ ○

_____ ○ ○ ○ ○ ○ ○ ○

_____ ○ ○ ○ ○ ○ ○ ○

NOTE:

My Weekly Planner

DATE:

MOON PHASE: NEW MOON / WAXING / FULL MOON / WANING

FOCUS: REST. REFLECT. SET INTENTION   / PLAN. INITIATE. ACTION

CONNECT. BE SEEN. RELEASE / COMPLETE. DELIVER. LET GO

TOP 3 PRIORITIES: **REMINDER:**

TO-DO LIST:

Weekly Schedule
Appointments / Workout / Meals

Date:

Monday

Tuesday

Wednesday

Thursday

Friday

Saturday

Sunday

Note

Weekly Check-In

DATE:

MOON PHASE:

CYCLE: Menstrual / Follicular / Ovulation / Luteal

MOOD:

BODY
How's your energy this week?

MIND
What is on your mind?

SPIRIT
How are you feeling?

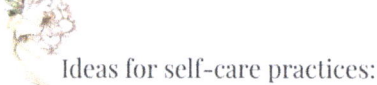

Ideas for self-care practices:

Habit Tracker

KEY FOCUS FOR THIS WEEK:

MY GOOD HABITS   M   T   W   TH   F   S   S

_____ ○ ○ ○ ○ ○ ○ ○

_____ ○ ○ ○ ○ ○ ○ ○

_____ ○ ○ ○ ○ ○ ○ ○

_____ ○ ○ ○ ○ ○ ○ ○

_____ ○ ○ ○ ○ ○ ○ ○

_____ ○ ○ ○ ○ ○ ○ ○

_____ ○ ○ ○ ○ ○ ○ ○

_____ ○ ○ ○ ○ ○ ○ ○

NOTE:

M	T	W	T	F	S	S

Turning It Over

My To-Do List   Universe To-Do List

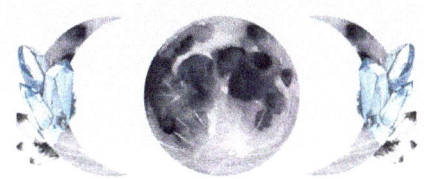

New Moon Intentions

Full Moon Release

My Weekly Planner

DATE:

MOON PHASE: NEW MOON / WAXING / FULL MOON / WANING

FOCUS: REST. REFLECT. SET INTENTION / PLAN. INITIATE. ACTION
CONNECT. BE SEEN. RELEASE / COMPLETE. DELIVER. LET GO

TOP 3 PRIORITIES: **REMINDER:**

TO-DO LIST:

Weekly Schedule
Appointments / Workout / Meals

Date:

Monday

Tuesday

Wednesday

Thursday

Friday

Saturday

Sunday

Note

Weekly Check-In

DATE:

MOON PHASE:

CYCLE: Menstrual / Follicular / Ovulation / Luteal

MOOD:

BODY
How's your energy this week?

MIND
What is on your mind?

SPIRIT
How are you feeling?

Ideas for self-care practices:

Habit Tracker

KEY FOCUS FOR THIS WEEK:

MY GOOD HABITS   M   T   W   TH   F   S   S

NOTE:

My Weekly Planner

DATE:

MOON PHASE: NEW MOON / WAXING / FULL MOON / WANING

FOCUS: REST. REFLECT. SET INTENTION   / PLAN. INITIATE. ACTION
    CONNECT. BE SEEN. RELEASE / COMPLETE. DELIVER. LET GO

TOP 3 PRIORITIES: **REMINDER:**

TO-DO LIST:

Weekly Schedule
Appointments / Workout / Meals

Date:

Monday

Tuesday

Wednesday

Thursday

Friday

Saturday

Sunday

Note

Weekly Check-In

DATE:

MOON PHASE:

CYCLE: Menstrual / Follicular / Ovulation / Luteal

MOOD:

BODY
How's your energy this week?

MIND
What is on your mind?

SPIRIT
How are you feeling?

Ideas for self-care practices:

Habit Tracker

KEY FOCUS FOR THIS WEEK:

MY GOOD HABITS	M	T	W	TH	F	S	S
_____	○	○	○	○	○	○	○
_____	○	○	○	○	○	○	○
_____	○	○	○	○	○	○	○
_____	○	○	○	○	○	○	○
_____	○	○	○	○	○	○	○
_____	○	○	○	○	○	○	○
_____	○	○	○	○	○	○	○
_____	○	○	○	○	○	○	○

NOTE:

My Weekly Planner

DATE:

MOON PHASE: NEW MOON / WAXING / FULL MOON / WANING

FOCUS: REST. REFLECT. SET INTENTION / PLAN. INITIATE. ACTION
CONNECT. BE SEEN. RELEASE / COMPLETE. DELIVER. LET GO

TOP 3 PRIORITIES: **REMINDER:**

TO-DO LIST:

Weekly Schedule
Appointments / Workout / Meals

Date:

Monday

Tuesday

Wednesday

Thursday

Friday

Saturday

Sunday

Note

Weekly Check-In

DATE:

MOON PHASE:

CYCLE: Menstrual / Follicular / Ovulation / Luteal

MOOD:

BODY
How's your energy this week?

MIND
What is on your mind?

SPIRIT
How are you feeling?

Ideas for self-care practices:

Habit Tracker

KEY FOCUS FOR THIS WEEK:

MY GOOD HABITS   M   T   W   TH   F   S   S

_____ ○ ○ ○ ○ ○ ○ ○

_____ ○ ○ ○ ○ ○ ○ ○

_____ ○ ○ ○ ○ ○ ○ ○

_____ ○ ○ ○ ○ ○ ○ ○

_____ ○ ○ ○ ○ ○ ○ ○

_____ ○ ○ ○ ○ ○ ○ ○

_____ ○ ○ ○ ○ ○ ○ ○

_____ ○ ○ ○ ○ ○ ○ ○

NOTE:

My Weekly Planner

DATE:

MOON PHASE: NEW MOON / WAXING / FULL MOON / WANING

FOCUS: REST. REFLECT. SET INTENTION   / PLAN. INITIATE. ACTION

CONNECT. BE SEEN. RELEASE / COMPLETE. DELIVER. LET GO

TOP 3 PRIORITIES: **REMINDER:**

TO-DO LIST:

Weekly Schedule
Appointments / Workout / Meals

Date:

Monday

Tuesday

Wednesday

Thursday

Friday

Saturday

Sunday

Note

Weekly Check-In

DATE:

MOON PHASE:

CYCLE: Menstrual / Follicular / Ovulation / Luteal

MOOD:

BODY
How's your energy this week?

MIND
What is on your mind?

SPIRIT
How are you feeling?

Ideas for self-care practices:

Habit Tracker

KEY FOCUS FOR THIS WEEK:

MY GOOD HABITS   M   T   W   TH   F   S   S

NOTE:

M　　　T　　　W　　　T　　　F　　　S　　　S

Turning It Over

My To-Do List **Universe To-Do List**

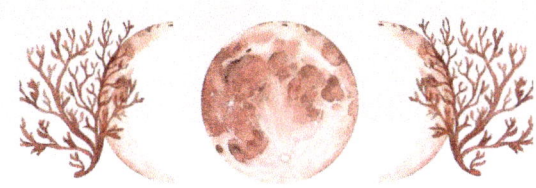

New Moon Intentions

Full Moon Release

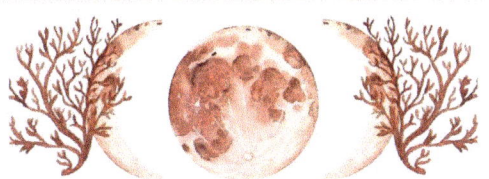

My Weekly Planner

DATE:

MOON PHASE: NEW MOON / WAXING / FULL MOON / WANING

FOCUS: REST. REFLECT. SET INTENTION / PLAN. INITIATE. ACTION
           CONNECT. BE SEEN. RELEASE / COMPLETE. DELIVER. LET GO

TOP 3 PRIORITIES: **REMINDER:**

TO-DO LIST:

Weekly Schedule

Appointments / Workout / Meals

Date:

Monday

Tuesday

Wednesday

Thursday

Friday

Saturday

Sunday

Note

Weekly Check-In

DATE:

MOON PHASE:

CYCLE: Menstrual / Follicular / Ovulation / Luteal

MOOD:

BODY
How's your energy this week?

MIND
What is on your mind?

SPIRIT
How are you feeling?

Ideas for self-care practices:

Habit Tracker

KEY FOCUS FOR THIS WEEK:

MY GOOD HABITS   M   T   W   TH   F   S   S

NOTE:

My Weekly Planner

DATE:

MOON PHASE: NEW MOON / WAXING / FULL MOON / WANING

FOCUS: REST. REFLECT. SET INTENTION / PLAN. INITIATE. ACTION
CONNECT. BE SEEN. RELEASE / COMPLETE. DELIVER. LET GO

TOP 3 PRIORITIES: **REMINDER:**

TO-DO LIST:

Weekly Schedule
Appointments / Workout / Meals

Date:

Monday

Tuesday

Wednesday

Thursday

Friday

Saturday

Sunday

Note

Weekly Check-In

DATE:

MOON PHASE:

CYCLE: Menstrual / Follicular / Ovulation / Luteal

MOOD:

BODY
How's your energy this week?

MIND
What is on your mind?

SPIRIT
How are you feeling?

Ideas for self-care practices:

Habit Tracker

KEY FOCUS FOR THIS WEEK:

MY GOOD HABITS   M   T   W   TH   F   S   S

NOTE:

My Weekly Planner

DATE:

MOON PHASE: NEW MOON / WAXING / FULL MOON / WANING

FOCUS: REST. REFLECT. SET INTENTION / PLAN. INITIATE. ACTION
CONNECT. BE SEEN. RELEASE / COMPLETE. DELIVER. LET GO

TOP 3 PRIORITIES: **REMINDER:**

TO-DO LIST:

Weekly Schedule
Appointments / Workout / Meals

Date:

Monday

Tuesday

Wednesday

Thursday

Friday

Saturday

Sunday

Note

Weekly Check-In

DATE:

MOON PHASE:

CYCLE: Menstrual / Follicular / Ovulation / Luteal

MOOD:

BODY
How's your energy this week?

MIND
What is on your mind?

SPIRIT
How are you feeling?

Ideas for self-care practices:

Habit Tracker

KEY FOCUS FOR THIS WEEK:

MY GOOD HABITS   M   T   W   TH   F   S   S

_____ ◯ ◯ ◯ ◯ ◯ ◯ ◯

_____ ◯ ◯ ◯ ◯ ◯ ◯ ◯

_____ ◯ ◯ ◯ ◯ ◯ ◯ ◯

_____ ◯ ◯ ◯ ◯ ◯ ◯ ◯

_____ ◯ ◯ ◯ ◯ ◯ ◯ ◯

_____ ◯ ◯ ◯ ◯ ◯ ◯ ◯

_____ ◯ ◯ ◯ ◯ ◯ ◯ ◯

_____ ◯ ◯ ◯ ◯ ◯ ◯ ◯

NOTE:

My Weekly Planner

DATE:

MOON PHASE: NEW MOON / WAXING / FULL MOON / WANING

FOCUS: REST. REFLECT. SET INTENTION   / PLAN. INITIATE. ACTION
CONNECT. BE SEEN. RELEASE / COMPLETE. DELIVER. LET GO

TOP 3 PRIORITIES: **REMINDER:**

TO-DO LIST:

Weekly Schedule

Appointments / Workout / Meals

Date:

Monday

Tuesday

Wednesday

Thursday

Friday

Saturday

Sunday

Note

Weekly Check-In

DATE:

MOON PHASE:

CYCLE: Menstrual / Follicular / Ovulation / Luteal

MOOD:

BODY
How's your energy this week?

MIND
What is on your mind?

SPIRIT
How are you feeling?

Ideas for self-care practices:

Habit Tracker

KEY FOCUS FOR THIS WEEK:

MY GOOD HABITS   M   T   W   TH   F   S   S

_____

_____

_____

_____

_____

_____

_____

_____

NOTE:

My Weekly Planner

DATE:

MOON PHASE: NEW MOON / WAXING / FULL MOON / WANING

FOCUS: REST. REFLECT. SET INTENTION / PLAN. INITIATE. ACTION

CONNECT. BE SEEN. RELEASE / COMPLETE. DELIVER. LET GO

TOP 3 PRIORITIES: **REMINDER:**

TO-DO LIST:

Weekly Schedule
Appointments / Workout / Meals

Date:

Monday

Tuesday

Wednesday

Thursday

Friday

Saturday

Sunday

Note

Weekly Check-In

DATE:

MOON PHASE:

CYCLE: Menstrual / Follicular / Ovulation / Luteal

MOOD:

BODY
How's your energy this week?

MIND
What is on your mind?

SPIRIT
How are you feeling?

Ideas for self-care practices:

Habit Tracker

KEY FOCUS FOR THIS WEEK:

MY GOOD HABITS   M   T   W   TH   F   S   S

NOTE:

M	T	W	T	F	S	S

Turning It Over

My To-Do List   Universe To-Do List

New Moon Intentions

Full Moon Release

My Weekly Planner

DATE:

MOON PHASE: NEW MOON / WAXING / FULL MOON / WANING

FOCUS: REST. REFLECT. SET INTENTION   / PLAN. INITIATE. ACTION
            CONNECT. BE SEEN. RELEASE / COMPLETE. DELIVER. LET GO

TOP 3 PRIORITIES: **REMINDER:**

TO-DO LIST:

Weekly Schedule
Appointments / Workout / Meals

Date:

Monday

Tuesday

Wednesday

Thursday

Friday

Saturday

Sunday

Note

Weekly Check-In

DATE:

MOON PHASE:

CYCLE: Menstrual / Follicular / Ovulation / Luteal

MOOD:

BODY
How's your energy this week?

MIND
What is on your mind?

SPIRIT
How are you feeling?

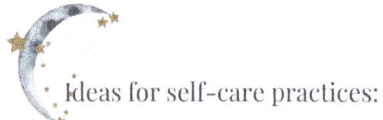

Ideas for self-care practices:

Habit Tracker

KEY FOCUS FOR THIS WEEK:

MY GOOD HABITS	M	T	W	TH	F	S	S
_____	○	○	○	○	○	○	○
_____	○	○	○	○	○	○	○
_____	○	○	○	○	○	○	○
_____	○	○	○	○	○	○	○
_____	○	○	○	○	○	○	○
_____	○	○	○	○	○	○	○
_____	○	○	○	○	○	○	○
_____	○	○	○	○	○	○	○

NOTE:

My Weekly Planner

DATE:

MOON PHASE: NEW MOON / WAXING / FULL MOON / WANING

FOCUS: REST. REFLECT. SET INTENTION / PLAN. INITIATE. ACTION
CONNECT. BE SEEN. RELEASE / COMPLETE. DELIVER. LET GO

TOP 3 PRIORITIES: **REMINDER:**

TO-DO LIST:

Weekly Schedule
Appointments / Workout / Meals

Date:

Monday

Tuesday

Wednesday

Thursday

Friday

Saturday

Sunday

Note

Weekly Check-In

DATE:

MOON PHASE:

CYCLE: Menstrual / Follicular / Ovulation / Luteal

MOOD:

BODY
How's your energy this week?

MIND
What is on your mind?

SPIRIT
How are you feeling?

Ideas for self-care practices:

Habit Tracker

KEY FOCUS FOR THIS WEEK:

MY GOOD HABITS   M   T   W   TH   F   S   S

NOTE:

My Weekly Planner

DATE:

MOON PHASE: NEW MOON / WAXING / FULL MOON / WANING

FOCUS: REST. REFLECT. SET INTENTION / PLAN. INITIATE. ACTION
CONNECT. BE SEEN. RELEASE / COMPLETE. DELIVER. LET GO

TOP 3 PRIORITIES: **REMINDER:**

TO-DO LIST:

Weekly Schedule

Appointments / Workout / Meals

Date:

Monday

Tuesday

Wednesday

Thursday

Friday

Saturday

Sunday

Note

Weekly Check-In

DATE:

MOON PHASE:

CYCLE: Menstrual / Follicular / Ovulation / Luteal

MOOD:

BODY
How's your energy this week?

MIND
What is on your mind?

SPIRIT
How are you feeling?

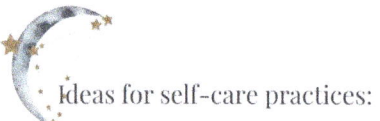

Ideas for self-care practices:

Habit Tracker

KEY FOCUS FOR THIS WEEK:

MY GOOD HABITS	M	T	W	TH	F	S	S
_____	○	○	○	○	○	○	○
_____	○	○	○	○	○	○	○
_____	○	○	○	○	○	○	○
_____	○	○	○	○	○	○	○
_____	○	○	○	○	○	○	○
_____	○	○	○	○	○	○	○
_____	○	○	○	○	○	○	○
_____	○	○	○	○	○	○	○

NOTE:

My Weekly Planner

DATE:

MOON PHASE: NEW MOON / WAXING / FULL MOON / WANING

FOCUS: REST. REFLECT. SET INTENTION / PLAN. INITIATE. ACTION
CONNECT. BE SEEN. RELEASE / COMPLETE. DELIVER. LET GO

TOP 3 PRIORITIES: **REMINDER:**

TO-DO LIST:

Weekly Schedule

Appointments / Workout / Meals

Date:

Monday

Tuesday

Wednesday

Thursday

Friday

Saturday

Sunday

Note

Weekly Check-In

DATE:

MOON PHASE:

CYCLE: Menstrual / Follicular / Ovulation / Luteal

MOOD:

BODY
How's your energy this week?

MIND
What is on your mind?

SPIRIT
How are you feeling?

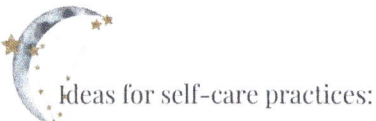

Ideas for self-care practices:

Habit Tracker

KEY FOCUS FOR THIS WEEK:

MY GOOD HABITS   M   T   W   TH   F   S   S

_____ ○ ○ ○ ○ ○ ○ ○

_____ ○ ○ ○ ○ ○ ○ ○

_____ ○ ○ ○ ○ ○ ○ ○

_____ ○ ○ ○ ○ ○ ○ ○

_____ ○ ○ ○ ○ ○ ○ ○

_____ ○ ○ ○ ○ ○ ○ ○

_____ ○ ○ ○ ○ ○ ○ ○

_____ ○ ○ ○ ○ ○ ○ ○

NOTE:

M	T	W	T	F	S	S

Turning It Over

My To-Do List   Universe To-Do List

New Moon Intentions

Full Moon Release

My Weekly Planner

DATE:

MOON PHASE: NEW MOON / WAXING / FULL MOON / WANING

FOCUS: REST. REFLECT. SET INTENTION   / PLAN. INITIATE. ACTION
           CONNECT. BE SEEN. RELEASE / COMPLETE. DELIVER. LET GO

TOP 3 PRIORITIES: **REMINDER:**

TO-DO LIST:

Weekly Schedule
Appointments / Workout / Meals

Date:

Monday

Tuesday

Wednesday

Thursday

Friday

Saturday

Sunday

Note

Weekly Check-In

DATE:

MOON PHASE:

CYCLE: Menstrual / Follicular / Ovulation / Luteal

MOOD:

BODY
How's your energy this week?

MIND
What is on your mind?

SPIRIT
How are you feeling?

Ideas for self-care practices:

Habit Tracker

KEY FOCUS FOR THIS WEEK:

MY GOOD HABITS   M   T   W   TH   F   S   S

NOTE:

My Weekly Planner

DATE:

MOON PHASE: NEW MOON / WAXING / FULL MOON/ WANING

FOCUS: REST. REFLECT. SET INTENTION   / PLAN. INITIATE. ACTION
           CONNECT. BE SEEN. RELEASE / COMPLETE. DELIVER. LET GO

TOP 3 PRIORITIES: **REMINDER:**

TO-DO LIST:

Weekly Schedule

Appointments / Workout / Meals

Date:

Monday

Tuesday

Wednesday

Thursday

Friday

Saturday

Sunday

Note

Weekly Check-In

DATE:

MOON PHASE:

CYCLE: Menstrual / Follicular / Ovulation / Luteal

MOOD:

BODY
How's your energy this week?

MIND
What is on your mind?

SPIRIT
How are you feeling?

Ideas for self-care practices:

KEY FOCUS FOR THIS WEEK:

MY GOOD HABITS   M   T   W   TH   F   S   S

_____

_____

_____

_____

_____

_____

_____

_____

NOTE:

My Weekly Planner

DATE:

MOON PHASE: NEW MOON / WAXING / FULL MOON / WANING

FOCUS: REST. REFLECT. SET INTENTION   / PLAN. INITIATE. ACTION
         CONNECT. BE SEEN. RELEASE / COMPLETE. DELIVER. LET GO

TOP 3 PRIORITIES: **REMINDER:**

TO-DO LIST:

Weekly Schedule

Appointments / Workout / Meals

Date:

Monday

Tuesday

Wednesday

Thursday

Friday

Saturday

Sunday

Note

Weekly Check-In

DATE:

MOON PHASE:

CYCLE: Menstrual / Follicular / Ovulation / Luteal

MOOD:

BODY
How's your energy this week?

MIND
What is on your mind?

SPIRIT
How are you feeling?

Ideas for self-care practices:

Habit Tracker

KEY FOCUS FOR THIS WEEK:

MY GOOD HABITS   M   T   W   TH   F   S   S

_____ ◯ ◯ ◯ ◯ ◯ ◯ ◯

_____ ◯ ◯ ◯ ◯ ◯ ◯ ◯

_____ ◯ ◯ ◯ ◯ ◯ ◯ ◯

_____ ◯ ◯ ◯ ◯ ◯ ◯ ◯

_____ ◯ ◯ ◯ ◯ ◯ ◯ ◯

_____ ◯ ◯ ◯ ◯ ◯ ◯ ◯

_____ ◯ ◯ ◯ ◯ ◯ ◯ ◯

_____ ◯ ◯ ◯ ◯ ◯ ◯ ◯

NOTE:

My Weekly Planner

DATE:

MOON PHASE: NEW MOON / WAXING / FULL MOON / WANING

FOCUS: REST. REFLECT. SET INTENTION / PLAN. INITIATE. ACTION
CONNECT. BE SEEN. RELEASE / COMPLETE. DELIVER. LET GO

TOP 3 PRIORITIES: **REMINDER:**

TO-DO LIST:

Weekly Schedule
Appointments / Workout / Meals

Date:

Monday

Tuesday

Wednesday

Thursday

Friday

Saturday

Sunday

Note

Weekly Check-In

DATE:

MOON PHASE:

CYCLE: Menstrual / Follicular / Ovulation / Luteal

MOOD:

BODY
How's your energy this week?

MIND
What is on your mind?

SPIRIT
How are you feeling?

Ideas for self-care practices:

Habit Tracker

KEY FOCUS FOR THIS WEEK:

MY GOOD HABITS   M   T   W   TH   F   S   S

_____   ○ ○ ○ ○ ○ ○ ○

_____   ○ ○ ○ ○ ○ ○ ○

_____   ○ ○ ○ ○ ○ ○ ○

_____   ○ ○ ○ ○ ○ ○ ○

_____   ○ ○ ○ ○ ○ ○ ○

_____   ○ ○ ○ ○ ○ ○ ○

_____   ○ ○ ○ ○ ○ ○ ○

_____   ○ ○ ○ ○ ○ ○ ○

NOTE:

My Weekly Planner

DATE:

MOON PHASE: NEW MOON / WAXING / FULL MOON / WANING

FOCUS: REST. REFLECT. SET INTENTION / PLAN. INITIATE. ACTION
             CONNECT. BE SEEN. RELEASE / COMPLETE. DELIVER. LET GO

TOP 3 PRIORITIES: **REMINDER:**

TO-DO LIST:

Weekly Schedule
Appointments / Workout / Meals

Date:

Monday

Tuesday

Wednesday

Thursday

Friday

Saturday

Sunday

Note

Weekly Check-In

DATE:

MOON PHASE:

CYCLE: Menstrual / Follicular / Ovulation / Luteal

MOOD:

BODY
How's your energy this week?

MIND
What is on your mind?

SPIRIT
How are you feeling?

Ideas for self-care practices:

Habit Tracker

KEY FOCUS FOR THIS WEEK:

MY GOOD HABITS   M   T   W   TH   F   S   S

_____

_____

_____

_____

_____

_____

_____

_____

NOTE:

M	T	W	T	F	S	S

Turning It Over

My To-Do List   **Universe To-Do List**

New Moon Intentions

Full Moon Release

My Weekly Planner

DATE:

MOON PHASE: NEW MOON / WAXING / FULL MOON / WANING

FOCUS: REST. REFLECT. SET INTENTION / PLAN. INITIATE. ACTION
CONNECT. BE SEEN. RELEASE / COMPLETE. DELIVER. LET GO

TOP 3 PRIORITIES: **REMINDER:**

TO-DO LIST:

Weekly Schedule
Appointments / Workout / Meals

Date:

Monday

Tuesday

Wednesday

Thursday

Friday

Saturday

Sunday

Note

Weekly Check-In

DATE:

MOON PHASE:

CYCLE: Menstrual / Follicular / Ovulation / Luteal

MOOD:

BODY
How's your energy this week?

MIND
What is on your mind?

SPIRIT
How are you feeling?

Ideas for self-care practices:

Habit Tracker

KEY FOCUS FOR THIS WEEK:

MY GOOD HABITS   M   T   W   TH   F   S   S

NOTE:

My Weekly Planner

DATE:

MOON PHASE: NEW MOON / WAXING / FULL MOON / WANING

FOCUS: REST. REFLECT. SET INTENTION / PLAN. INITIATE. ACTION
CONNECT. BE SEEN. RELEASE / COMPLETE. DELIVER. LET GO

TOP 3 PRIORITIES: **REMINDER:**

TO-DO LIST:

Weekly Schedule
Appointments / Workout / Meals

Date:

Monday

Tuesday

Wednesday

Thursday

Friday

Saturday

Sunday

Note

Weekly Check-In

DATE:

MOON PHASE:

CYCLE: Menstrual / Follicular / Ovulation / Luteal

MOOD:

BODY
How's your energy this week?

MIND
What is on your mind?

SPIRIT
How are you feeling?

Ideas for self-care practices:

Habit Tracker

KEY FOCUS FOR THIS WEEK:

MY GOOD HABITS	M	T	W	TH	F	S	S
_____	○	○	○	○	○	○	○
_____	○	○	○	○	○	○	○
_____	○	○	○	○	○	○	○
_____	○	○	○	○	○	○	○
_____	○	○	○	○	○	○	○
_____	○	○	○	○	○	○	○
_____	○	○	○	○	○	○	○
_____	○	○	○	○	○	○	○

NOTE:

My Weekly Planner

DATE:

MOON PHASE: NEW MOON / WAXING / FULL MOON / WANING

FOCUS: REST. REFLECT. SET INTENTION   / PLAN. INITIATE. ACTION

CONNECT. BE SEEN. RELEASE / COMPLETE. DELIVER. LET GO

TOP 3 PRIORITIES: **REMINDER:**

TO-DO LIST:

Weekly Schedule
Appointments / Workout / Meals

Date:

Monday

Tuesday

Wednesday

Thursday

Friday

Saturday

Sunday

Note

Weekly Check-In

DATE:

MOON PHASE:

CYCLE: Menstrual / Follicular / Ovulation / Luteal

MOOD:

BODY
How's your energy this week?

MIND
What is on your mind?

SPIRIT
How are you feeling?

Ideas for self-care practices:

Habit Tracker

KEY FOCUS FOR THIS WEEK:

MY GOOD HABITS   M   T   W   TH   F   S   S

_____ ◯ ◯ ◯ ◯ ◯ ◯ ◯

_____ ◯ ◯ ◯ ◯ ◯ ◯ ◯

_____ ◯ ◯ ◯ ◯ ◯ ◯ ◯

_____ ◯ ◯ ◯ ◯ ◯ ◯ ◯

_____ ◯ ◯ ◯ ◯ ◯ ◯ ◯

_____ ◯ ◯ ◯ ◯ ◯ ◯ ◯

_____ ◯ ◯ ◯ ◯ ◯ ◯ ◯

_____ ◯ ◯ ◯ ◯ ◯ ◯ ◯

NOTE:

My Weekly Planner

DATE:

MOON PHASE: NEW MOON / WAXING / FULL MOON / WANING

FOCUS: REST. REFLECT. SET INTENTION   / PLAN. INITIATE. ACTION

   CONNECT. BE SEEN. RELEASE / COMPLETE. DELIVER. LET GO

TOP 3 PRIORITIES: **REMINDER:**

TO-DO LIST:

Weekly Schedule
Appointments / Workout / Meals

Date:

Monday

Tuesday

Wednesday

Thursday

Friday

Saturday

Sunday

Note

Weekly Check-In

DATE:

MOON PHASE:

CYCLE: Menstrual / Follicular / Ovulation / Luteal

MOOD:

BODY
How's your energy this week?

MIND
What is on your mind?

SPIRIT
How are you feeling?

Ideas for self-care practices:

Habit Tracker

KEY FOCUS FOR THIS WEEK:

MY GOOD HABITS   M   T   W   TH   F   S   S

NOTE:

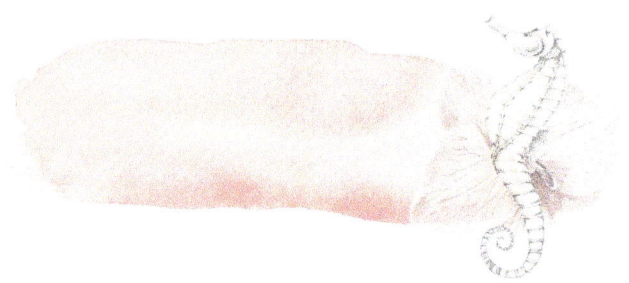

M T W T F S S

Turning It Over

My To-Do List **Universe To-Do List**

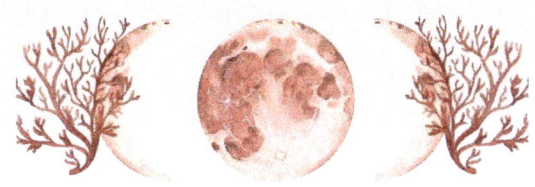

New Moon Intentions

Full Moon Release

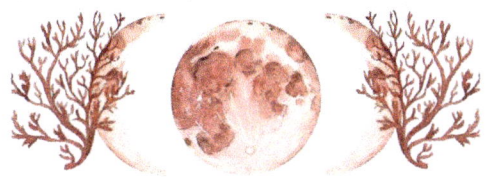

My Weekly Planner

DATE:

MOON PHASE: NEW MOON / WAXING / FULL MOON / WANING

FOCUS: REST. REFLECT. SET INTENTION / PLAN. INITIATE. ACTION

CONNECT. BE SEEN. RELEASE / COMPLETE. DELIVER. LET GO

TOP 3 PRIORITIES: **REMINDER:**

TO-DO LIST:

Weekly Schedule
Appointments / Workout / Meals

Date:

Monday

Tuesday

Wednesday

Thursday

Friday

Saturday

Sunday

Note

Weekly Check-In

DATE:

MOON PHASE:

CYCLE: Menstrual / Follicular / Ovulation / Luteal

MOOD:

BODY
How's your energy this week?

MIND
What is on your mind?

SPIRIT
How are you feeling?

Ideas for self-care practices:

Habit Tracker

KEY FOCUS FOR THIS WEEK:

MY GOOD HABITS   M   T   W   TH   F   S   S

NOTE:

My Weekly Planner

DATE:

MOON PHASE: NEW MOON / WAXING / FULL MOON / WANING

FOCUS: REST. REFLECT. SET INTENTION   / PLAN. INITIATE. ACTION
         CONNECT. BE SEEN. RELEASE / COMPLETE. DELIVER. LET GO

TOP 3 PRIORITIES: **REMINDER:**

TO-DO LIST:

Weekly Schedule
Appointments / Workout / Meals

Date:

Monday

Tuesday

Wednesday

Thursday

Friday

Saturday

Sunday

Note

Weekly Check-In

DATE:

MOON PHASE:

CYCLE: Menstrual / Follicular / Ovulation / Luteal

MOOD:

BODY
How's your energy this week?

MIND
What is on your mind?

SPIRIT
How are you feeling?

Ideas for self-care practices:

Habit Tracker

KEY FOCUS FOR THIS WEEK:

MY GOOD HABITS   M   T   W   TH   F   S   S

NOTE:

My Weekly Planner

DATE:

MOON PHASE: NEW MOON / WAXING / FULL MOON / WANING

FOCUS: REST. REFLECT. SET INTENTION / PLAN. INITIATE. ACTION
CONNECT. BE SEEN. RELEASE / COMPLETE. DELIVER. LET GO

TOP 3 PRIORITIES: **REMINDER:**

TO-DO LIST:

Weekly Schedule
Appointments / Workout / Meals

Date:

Monday

Tuesday

Wednesday

Thursday

Friday

Saturday

Sunday

Note

Weekly Check-In

DATE:

MOON PHASE:

CYCLE: Menstrual / Follicular / Ovulation / Luteal

MOOD:

BODY
How's your energy this week?

MIND
What is on your mind?

SPIRIT
How are you feeling?

Ideas for self-care practices:

Habit Tracker

KEY FOCUS FOR THIS WEEK:

MY GOOD HABITS   M   T   W   TH   F   S   S

NOTE:

My Weekly Planner

DATE:

MOON PHASE: NEW MOON / WAXING / FULL MOON / WANING

FOCUS: REST. REFLECT. SET INTENTION / PLAN. INITIATE. ACTION
CONNECT. BE SEEN. RELEASE / COMPLETE. DELIVER. LET GO

TOP 3 PRIORITIES: **REMINDER:**

TO-DO LIST:

Weekly Schedule

Appointments / Workout / Meals

Date:

Monday

Tuesday

Wednesday

Thursday

Friday

Saturday

Sunday

Note

Weekly Check-In

DATE:

MOON PHASE:

CYCLE: Menstrual / Follicular / Ovulation / Luteal

MOOD:

BODY
How's your energy this week?

MIND
What is on your mind?

SPIRIT
How are you feeling?

Ideas for self-care practices:

Habit Tracker

KEY FOCUS FOR THIS WEEK:

MY GOOD HABITS   M   T   W   TH   F   S   S

_____ ◯ ◯ ◯ ◯ ◯ ◯ ◯

_____ ◯ ◯ ◯ ◯ ◯ ◯ ◯

_____ ◯ ◯ ◯ ◯ ◯ ◯ ◯

_____ ◯ ◯ ◯ ◯ ◯ ◯ ◯

_____ ◯ ◯ ◯ ◯ ◯ ◯ ◯

_____ ◯ ◯ ◯ ◯ ◯ ◯ ◯

_____ ◯ ◯ ◯ ◯ ◯ ◯ ◯

_____ ◯ ◯ ◯ ◯ ◯ ◯ ◯

NOTE:

My Weekly Planner

DATE:

MOON PHASE: NEW MOON / WAXING / FULL MOON / WANING

FOCUS: REST. REFLECT. SET INTENTION / PLAN. INITIATE. ACTION

CONNECT. BE SEEN. RELEASE / COMPLETE. DELIVER. LET GO

TOP 3 PRIORITIES: **REMINDER:**

TO-DO LIST:

Weekly Schedule
Appointments / Workout / Meals

Date:

Monday

Tuesday

Wednesday

Thursday

Friday

Saturday

Sunday

Note

Weekly Check-In

DATE:

MOON PHASE:

CYCLE: Menstrual / Follicular / Ovulation / Luteal

MOOD:

BODY
How's your energy this week?

MIND
What is on your mind?

SPIRIT
How are you feeling?

Ideas for self-care practices:

Habit Tracker

KEY FOCUS FOR THIS WEEK:

MY GOOD HABITS   M   T   W   TH   F   S   S

NOTE:

M	T	W	T	F	S	S

Turning It Over

My To-Do List

Universe To-Do List

New Moon Intentions

Full Moon Release

My Weekly Planner

DATE:

MOON PHASE: NEW MOON / WAXING / FULL MOON / WANING

FOCUS: REST. REFLECT. SET INTENTION / PLAN. INITIATE. ACTION
CONNECT. BE SEEN. RELEASE / COMPLETE. DELIVER. LET GO

TOP 3 PRIORITIES: **REMINDER:**

TO-DO LIST:

Weekly Schedule

Appointments / Workout / Meals

Date:

Monday

Tuesday

Wednesday

Thursday

Friday

Saturday

Sunday

Note

Weekly Check-In

DATE:

MOON PHASE:

CYCLE: Menstrual / Follicular / Ovulation / Luteal

MOOD:

BODY
How's your energy this week?

MIND
What is on your mind?

SPIRIT
How are you feeling?

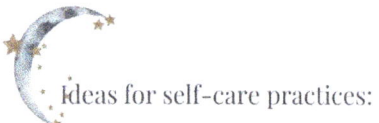

Ideas for self-care practices:

KEY FOCUS FOR THIS WEEK:

MY GOOD HABITS   M   T   W   TH   F   S   S

NOTE:

My Weekly Planner

DATE:

MOON PHASE: NEW MOON / WAXING / FULL MOON / WANING

FOCUS: REST. REFLECT. SET INTENTION   / PLAN. INITIATE. ACTION

CONNECT. BE SEEN. RELEASE / COMPLETE. DELIVER. LET GO

TOP 3 PRIORITIES: **REMINDER:**

TO-DO LIST:

Weekly Schedule
Appointments / Workout / Meals

Date:

Monday

Tuesday

Wednesday

Thursday

Friday

Saturday

Sunday

Note

Weekly Check-In

DATE:

MOON PHASE:

CYCLE: Menstrual / Follicular / Ovulation / Luteal

MOOD:

BODY
How's your energy this week?

MIND
What is on your mind?

SPIRIT
How are you feeling?

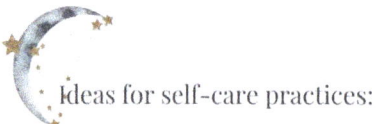

Ideas for self-care practices:

Habit Tracker

KEY FOCUS FOR THIS WEEK:

MY GOOD HABITS	M	T	W	TH	F	S	S
_____	○	○	○	○	○	○	○
_____	○	○	○	○	○	○	○
_____	○	○	○	○	○	○	○
_____	○	○	○	○	○	○	○
_____	○	○	○	○	○	○	○
_____	○	○	○	○	○	○	○
_____	○	○	○	○	○	○	○
_____	○	○	○	○	○	○	○

NOTE:

My Weekly Planner

DATE:

MOON PHASE: NEW MOON / WAXING / FULL MOON / WANING

FOCUS: REST. REFLECT. SET INTENTION / PLAN. INITIATE. ACTION
CONNECT. BE SEEN. RELEASE / COMPLETE. DELIVER. LET GO

TOP 3 PRIORITIES: **REMINDER:**

TO-DO LIST:

Weekly Schedule
Appointments / Workout / Meals

Date:

Monday

Tuesday

Wednesday

Thursday

Friday

Saturday

Sunday

Note

Weekly Check-In

DATE:

MOON PHASE:

CYCLE: Menstrual / Follicular / Ovulation / Luteal

MOOD:

BODY
How's your energy this week?

MIND
What is on your mind?

SPIRIT
How are you feeling?

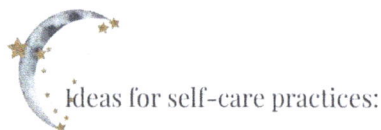

Ideas for self-care practices:

KEY FOCUS FOR THIS WEEK:

MY GOOD HABITS   M   T   W   TH   F   S   S

NOTE:

My Weekly Planner

DATE:

MOON PHASE: NEW MOON / WAXING / FULL MOON / WANING

FOCUS: REST. REFLECT. SET INTENTION   / PLAN. INITIATE. ACTION

CONNECT. BE SEEN. RELEASE / COMPLETE. DELIVER. LET GO

TOP 3 PRIORITIES: **REMINDER:**

TO-DO LIST:

Weekly Schedule
Appointments / Workout / Meals

Date:

Monday

Tuesday

Wednesday

Thursday

Friday

Saturday

Sunday

Note

Weekly Check-In

DATE:

MOON PHASE:

CYCLE: Menstrual / Follicular / Ovulation / Luteal

MOOD:

BODY
How's your energy this week?

MIND
What is on your mind?

SPIRIT
How are you feeling?

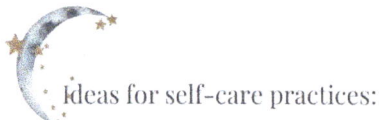
Ideas for self-care practices:

Habit Tracker

KEY FOCUS FOR THIS WEEK?

MY GOOD HABITS   M   T   W   TH   F   S   S

_____ ○ ○ ○ ○ ○ ○ ○

_____ ○ ○ ○ ○ ○ ○ ○

_____ ○ ○ ○ ○ ○ ○ ○

_____ ○ ○ ○ ○ ○ ○ ○

_____ ○ ○ ○ ○ ○ ○ ○

_____ ○ ○ ○ ○ ○ ○ ○

_____ ○ ○ ○ ○ ○ ○ ○

_____ ○ ○ ○ ○ ○ ○ ○

NOTE:

M	T	W	T	F	S	S

Turning It Over

My To-Do List   **Universe To-Do List**

New Moon Intentions

Full Moon Release

My Weekly Planner

DATE:

MOON PHASE: NEW MOON / WAXING / FULL MOON / WANING

FOCUS: REST. REFLECT. SET INTENTION   / PLAN. INITIATE. ACTION
           CONNECT. BE SEEN. RELEASE / COMPLETE. DELIVER. LET GO

TOP 3 PRIORITIES: **REMINDER:**

TO-DO LIST:

Weekly Schedule
Appointments / Workout / Meals

Date:

Monday

Tuesday

Wednesday

Thursday

Friday

Saturday

Sunday

Note

Weekly Check-In

DATE:

MOON PHASE:

CYCLE: Menstrual / Follicular / Ovulation / Luteal

MOOD:

BODY
How's your energy this week?

MIND
What is on your mind?

SPIRIT
How are you feeling?

Ideas for self-care practices:

Habit Tracker

KEY FOCUS FOR THIS WEEK:

MY GOOD HABITS   M   T   W   TH   F   S   S

_____ ◯ ◯ ◯ ◯ ◯ ◯ ◯

_____ ◯ ◯ ◯ ◯ ◯ ◯ ◯

_____ ◯ ◯ ◯ ◯ ◯ ◯ ◯

_____ ◯ ◯ ◯ ◯ ◯ ◯ ◯

_____ ◯ ◯ ◯ ◯ ◯ ◯ ◯

_____ ◯ ◯ ◯ ◯ ◯ ◯ ◯

_____ ◯ ◯ ◯ ◯ ◯ ◯ ◯

_____ ◯ ◯ ◯ ◯ ◯ ◯ ◯

NOTE:

My Weekly Planner

DATE:

MOON PHASE: NEW MOON / WAXING / FULL MOON / WANING

FOCUS: REST. REFLECT. SET INTENTION / PLAN. INITIATE. ACTION
CONNECT. BE SEEN. RELEASE / COMPLETE. DELIVER. LET GO

TOP 3 PRIORITIES: **REMINDER:**

TO-DO LIST:

Weekly Schedule

Appointments / Workout / Meals

Date:

Monday

Tuesday

Wednesday

Thursday

Friday

Saturday

Sunday

Note

Weekly Check-In

DATE:

MOON PHASE:

CYCLE: Menstrual / Follicular / Ovulation / Luteal

MOOD:

BODY
How's your energy this week?

MIND
What is on your mind?

SPIRIT
How are you feeling?

Ideas for self-care practices:

Habit Tracker

KEY FOCUS FOR THIS WEEK:

MY GOOD HABITS   M   T   W   TH   F   S   S

_____

_____

_____

_____

_____

_____

_____

_____

NOTE:

My Weekly Planner

DATE:

MOON PHASE: NEW MOON / WAXING / FULL MOON / WANING

FOCUS: REST. REFLECT. SET INTENTION / PLAN. INITIATE. ACTION
CONNECT. BE SEEN. RELEASE / COMPLETE. DELIVER. LET GO

TOP 3 PRIORITIES: **REMINDER:**

TO-DO LIST:

Weekly Schedule
Appointments / Workout / Meals

Date:

Monday

Tuesday

Wednesday

Thursday

Friday

Saturday

Sunday

Note

Weekly Check-In

DATE:

MOON PHASE:

CYCLE: Menstrual / Follicular / Ovulation / Luteal

MOOD:

BODY
How's your energy this week?

MIND
What is on your mind?

SPIRIT
How are you feeling?

Ideas for self-care practices:

Habit Tracker

KEY FOCUS FOR THIS WEEK:

MY GOOD HABITS   M   T   W   TH   F   S   S

NOTE:

My Weekly Planner

DATE:

MOON PHASE: NEW MOON / WAXING / FULL MOON / WANING

FOCUS: REST. REFLECT. SET INTENTION / PLAN. INITIATE. ACTION
CONNECT. BE SEEN. RELEASE / COMPLETE. DELIVER. LET GO

TOP 3 PRIORITIES: **REMINDER:**

TO-DO LIST:

Weekly Schedule

Appointments / Workout / Meals

Date:

Monday

Tuesday

Wednesday

Thursday

Friday

Saturday

Sunday

Note

Weekly Check-In

DATE:

MOON PHASE:

CYCLE: Menstrual / Follicular / Ovulation / Luteal

MOOD:

BODY
How's your energy this week?

MIND
What is on your mind?

SPIRIT
How are you feeling?

Ideas for self-care practices:

Habit Tracker

KEY FOCUS FOR THIS WEEK:

MY GOOD HABITS   M   T   W   TH   F   S   S

NOTE:

My Weekly Planner

DATE:

MOON PHASE: NEW MOON / WAXING / FULL MOON / WANING

FOCUS: REST. REFLECT. SET INTENTION / PLAN. INITIATE. ACTION
CONNECT. BE SEEN. RELEASE / COMPLETE. DELIVER. LET GO

TOP 3 PRIORITIES: **REMINDER:**

TO-DO LIST:

Weekly Schedule

Appointments / Workout / Meals

Date:

Monday

Tuesday

Wednesday

Thursday

Friday

Saturday

Sunday

Note

Weekly Check-In

DATE:

MOON PHASE:

CYCLE: Menstrual / Follicular / Ovulation / Luteal

MOOD:

BODY
How's your energy this week?

MIND
What is on your mind?

SPIRIT
How are you feeling?

Ideas for self-care practices:

Habit Tracker

KEY FOCUS FOR THIS WEEK:

MY GOOD HABITS   M   T   W   TH   F   S   S

_____ ○ ○ ○ ○ ○ ○ ○

_____ ○ ○ ○ ○ ○ ○ ○

_____ ○ ○ ○ ○ ○ ○ ○

_____ ○ ○ ○ ○ ○ ○ ○

_____ ○ ○ ○ ○ ○ ○ ○

_____ ○ ○ ○ ○ ○ ○ ○

_____ ○ ○ ○ ○ ○ ○ ○

_____ ○ ○ ○ ○ ○ ○ ○

NOTE:

M	T	W	T	F	S	S

Turning It Over

My To-Do List **Universe To-Do List**

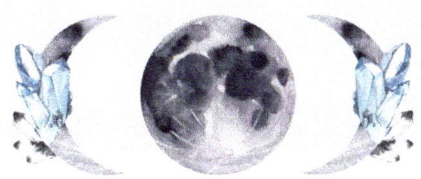

New Moon Intentions

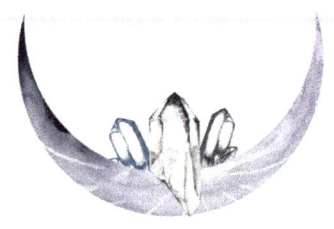

Full Moon Release

My Weekly Planner

DATE:

MOON PHASE: NEW MOON / WAXING / FULL MOON / WANING

FOCUS: REST. REFLECT. SET INTENTION / PLAN. INITIATE. ACTION
CONNECT. BE SEEN. RELEASE / COMPLETE. DELIVER. LET GO

TOP 3 PRIORITIES: **REMINDER:**

TO-DO LIST:

Weekly Schedule
Appointments / Workout / Meals

Date:

Monday

Tuesday

Wednesday

Thursday

Friday

Saturday

Sunday

Note

Weekly Check-In

DATE:

MOON PHASE:

CYCLE: Menstrual / Follicular / Ovulation / Luteal

MOOD:

BODY
How's your energy this week?

MIND
What is on your mind?

SPIRIT
How are you feeling?

Ideas for self-care practices:

Habit Tracker

KEY FOCUS FOR THIS WEEK:

MY GOOD HABITS   M   T   W   TH   F   S   S

_____ ○   ○   ○   ○   ○   ○   ○

_____ ○   ○   ○   ○   ○   ○   ○

_____ ○   ○   ○   ○   ○   ○   ○

_____ ○   ○   ○   ○   ○   ○   ○

_____ ○   ○   ○   ○   ○   ○   ○

_____ ○   ○   ○   ○   ○   ○   ○

_____ ○   ○   ○   ○   ○   ○   ○

_____ ○   ○   ○   ○   ○   ○   ○

NOTE:

My Weekly Planner

DATE:

MOON PHASE: NEW MOON / WAXING / FULL MOON / WANING

FOCUS: REST. REFLECT. SET INTENTION   / PLAN. INITIATE. ACTION
          CONNECT. BE SEEN. RELEASE / COMPLETE. DELIVER. LET GO

TOP 3 PRIORITIES: **REMINDER:**

TO-DO LIST:

Weekly Schedule
Appointments / Workout / Meals

Date:

Monday

Tuesday

Wednesday

Thursday

Friday

Saturday

Sunday

Note

Weekly Check-In

DATE:

MOON PHASE:

CYCLE: Menstrual / Follicular / Ovulation / Luteal

MOOD:

BODY
How's your energy this week?

MIND
What is on your mind?

SPIRIT
How are you feeling?

Ideas for self-care practices:

Habit Tracker

KEY FOCUS FOR THIS WEEK:

MY GOOD HABITS   M   T   W   TH   F   S   S

NOTE:

My Weekly Planner

DATE:

MOON PHASE: NEW MOON / WAXING / FULL MOON / WANING

FOCUS: REST. REFLECT. SET INTENTION   / PLAN. INITIATE. ACTION
CONNECT. BE SEEN. RELEASE / COMPLETE. DELIVER. LET GO

TOP 3 PRIORITIES: **REMINDER:**

TO-DO LIST:

Weekly Schedule
Appointments / Workout / Meals

Date:

Monday

Tuesday

Wednesday

Thursday

Friday

Saturday

Sunday

Note

Weekly Check-In

DATE:

MOON PHASE:

CYCLE: Menstrual / Follicular / Ovulation / Luteal

MOOD:

BODY
How's your energy this week?

MIND
What is on your mind?

SPIRIT
How are you feeling?

Ideas for self-care practices:

Habit Tracker

KEY FOCUS FOR THIS WEEK:

MY GOOD HABITS   M   T   W   TH   F   S   S

NOTE:

My Weekly Planner

DATE:

MOON PHASE: NEW MOON / WAXING / FULL MOON/ WANING

FOCUS: REST. REFLECT. SET INTENTION   / PLAN. INITIATE. ACTION

   CONNECT. BE SEEN. RELEASE / COMPLETE. DELIVER. LET GO

TOP 3 PRIORITIES: **REMINDER:**

TO-DO LIST:

Weekly Schedule
Appointments / Workout / Meals

Date:

Monday

Tuesday

Wednesday

Thursday

Friday

Saturday

Sunday

Note

Weekly Check-In

DATE:

MOON PHASE:

CYCLE: Menstrual / Follicular / Ovulation / Luteal

MOOD:

BODY
How's your energy this week?

MIND
What is on your mind?

SPIRIT
How are you feeling?

Ideas for self-care practices:

Habit Tracker

KEY FOCUS FOR THIS WEEK:

MY GOOD HABITS   M   T   W   TH   F   S   S

_____

_____

_____

_____

_____

_____

_____

_____

NOTE:

M	T	W	T	F	S	S

Turning It Over

My To-Do List   *Universe To-Do List*

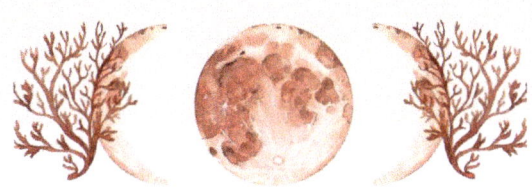

New Moon Intentions

Full Moon Release

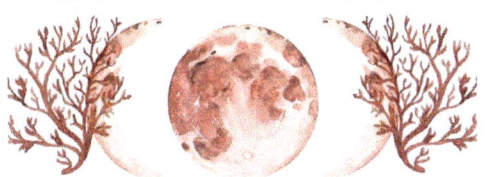

My Weekly Planner

DATE:

MOON PHASE: NEW MOON / WAXING / FULL MOON / WANING

FOCUS: REST. REFLECT. SET INTENTION / PLAN. INITIATE. ACTION
CONNECT. BE SEEN. RELEASE / COMPLETE. DELIVER. LET GO

TOP 3 PRIORITIES: **REMINDER:**

TO-DO LIST:

Weekly Schedule
Appointments / Workout / Meals

Date:

Monday

Tuesday

Wednesday

Thursday

Friday

Saturday

Sunday

Note

Weekly Check-In

DATE:

MOON PHASE:

CYCLE: Menstrual / Follicular / Ovulation / Luteal

MOOD:

BODY
How's your energy this week?

MIND
What is on your mind?

SPIRIT
How are you feeling?

Ideas for self-care practices:

Habit Tracker

KEY FOCUS FOR THIS WEEK:

MY GOOD HABITS   M   T   W   TH   F   S   S

_____

_____

_____

_____

_____

_____

_____

_____

NOTE:

My Weekly Planner

DATE:

MOON PHASE: NEW MOON / WAXING / FULL MOON / WANING

FOCUS: REST. REFLECT. SET INTENTION / PLAN. INITIATE. ACTION
CONNECT. BE SEEN. RELEASE / COMPLETE. DELIVER. LET GO

TOP 3 PRIORITIES: **REMINDER:**

TO-DO LIST:

Weekly Schedule

Appointments / Workout / Meals

Date:

Monday

Tuesday

Wednesday

Thursday

Friday

Saturday

Sunday

Note

Weekly Check-In

DATE:

MOON PHASE:

CYCLE: Menstrual / Follicular / Ovulation / Luteal

MOOD:

BODY
How's your energy this week?

MIND
What is on your mind?

SPIRIT
How are you feeling?

Ideas for self-care practices:

Habit Tracker

KEY FOCUS FOR THIS WEEK:

MY GOOD HABITS   M   T   W   TH   F   S   S

_____ ◯ ◯ ◯ ◯ ◯ ◯ ◯

_____ ◯ ◯ ◯ ◯ ◯ ◯ ◯

_____ ◯ ◯ ◯ ◯ ◯ ◯ ◯

_____ ◯ ◯ ◯ ◯ ◯ ◯ ◯

_____ ◯ ◯ ◯ ◯ ◯ ◯ ◯

_____ ◯ ◯ ◯ ◯ ◯ ◯ ◯

_____ ◯ ◯ ◯ ◯ ◯ ◯ ◯

_____ ◯ ◯ ◯ ◯ ◯ ◯ ◯

NOTE:

My Weekly Planner

DATE:

MOON PHASE: NEW MOON / WAXING / FULL MOON / WANING

FOCUS: REST. REFLECT. SET INTENTION   / PLAN. INITIATE. ACTION

   CONNECT. BE SEEN. RELEASE / COMPLETE. DELIVER. LET GO

TOP 3 PRIORITIES: **REMINDER:**

TO-DO LIST:

Weekly Schedule

Appointments / Workout / Meals

Date:

Monday

Tuesday

Wednesday

Thursday

Friday

Saturday

Sunday

Note

Weekly Check-In

DATE:

MOON PHASE:

CYCLE: Menstrual / Follicular / Ovulation / Luteal

MOOD:

BODY
How's your energy this week?

MIND
What is on your mind?

SPIRIT
How are you feeling?

Ideas for self-care practices:

Habit Tracker

KEY FOCUS FOR THIS WEEK:

MY GOOD HABITS	M	T	W	TH	F	S	S
_____	○	○	○	○	○	○	○
_____	○	○	○	○	○	○	○
_____	○	○	○	○	○	○	○
_____	○	○	○	○	○	○	○
_____	○	○	○	○	○	○	○
_____	○	○	○	○	○	○	○
_____	○	○	○	○	○	○	○
_____	○	○	○	○	○	○	○

NOTE:

My Weekly Planner

DATE:

MOON PHASE: NEW MOON / WAXING / FULL MOON / WANING

FOCUS: REST. REFLECT. SET INTENTION / PLAN. INITIATE. ACTION
CONNECT. BE SEEN. RELEASE / COMPLETE. DELIVER. LET GO

TOP 3 PRIORITIES: **REMINDER:**

TO-DO LIST:

Weekly Schedule
Appointments / Workout / Meals

Date:

Monday

Tuesday

Wednesday

Thursday

Friday

Saturday

Sunday

Note

Weekly Check-In

DATE:

MOON PHASE:

CYCLE: Menstrual / Follicular / Ovulation / Luteal

MOOD:

BODY
How's your energy this week?

MIND
What is on your mind?

SPIRIT
How are you feeling?

Ideas for self-care practices:

Habit Tracker

KEY FOCUS FOR THIS WEEK:

MY GOOD HABITS   M   T   W   TH   F   S   S

NOTE:

My Weekly Planner

DATE:

MOON PHASE: NEW MOON / WAXING / FULL MOON / WANING

FOCUS: REST. REFLECT. SET INTENTION / PLAN. INITIATE. ACTION
CONNECT. BE SEEN. RELEASE / COMPLETE. DELIVER. LET GO

TOP 3 PRIORITIES: **REMINDER:**

TO-DO LIST:

Weekly Schedule

Appointments / Workout / Meals

Date:

Monday

Tuesday

Wednesday

Thursday

Friday

Saturday

Sunday

Note

Weekly Check-In

DATE:

MOON PHASE:

CYCLE: Menstrual / Follicular / Ovulation / Luteal

MOOD:

BODY
How's your energy this week?

MIND
What is on your mind?

SPIRIT
How are you feeling?

Ideas for self-care practices:

Habit Tracker

KEY FOCUS FOR THIS WEEK:

MY GOOD HABITS   M   T   W   TH   F   S   S

_____

_____

_____

_____

_____

_____

_____

_____

NOTE:

M	T	W	T	F	S	S

Turning It Over

My To-Do List   Universe To-Do List

New Moon Intentions

Full Moon Release

My Weekly Planner

DATE:

MOON PHASE: NEW MOON / WAXING / FULL MOON / WANING

FOCUS: REST. REFLECT. SET INTENTION / PLAN. INITIATE. ACTION
CONNECT. BE SEEN. RELEASE / COMPLETE. DELIVER. LET GO

TOP 3 PRIORITIES: **REMINDER:**

TO-DO LIST:

Weekly Schedule
Appointments / Workout / Meals

Date:

Monday

Tuesday

Wednesday

Thursday

Friday

Saturday

Sunday

Note

Weekly Check-In

DATE:

MOON PHASE:

CYCLE: Menstrual / Follicular / Ovulation / Luteal

MOOD:

BODY
How's your energy this week?

MIND
What is on your mind?

SPIRIT
How are you feeling?

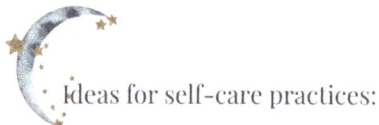

Ideas for self-care practices:

Habit Tracker

KEY FOCUS FOR THIS WEEK:

MY GOOD HABITS   M   T   W   TH   F   S   S

_____

_____

_____

_____

_____

_____

_____

_____

NOTE:

My Weekly Planner

DATE:

MOON PHASE: NEW MOON / WAXING / FULL MOON / WANING

FOCUS: REST. REFLECT. SET INTENTION / PLAN. INITIATE. ACTION
CONNECT. BE SEEN. RELEASE / COMPLETE. DELIVER. LET GO

TOP 3 PRIORITIES: **REMINDER:**

TO-DO LIST:

Weekly Schedule
Appointments / Workout / Meals

Date:

Monday

Tuesday

Wednesday

Thursday

Friday

Saturday

Sunday

Note

Weekly Check-In

DATE:

MOON PHASE:

CYCLE: Menstrual / Follicular / Ovulation / Luteal

MOOD:

BODY
How's your energy this week?

MIND
What is on your mind?

SPIRIT
How are you feeling?

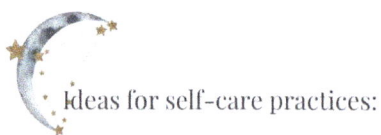
Ideas for self-care practices:

KEY FOCUS FOR THIS WEEK:

MY GOOD HABITS   M   T   W   TH   F   S   S

_____ ◯ ◯ ◯ ◯ ◯ ◯ ◯

_____ ◯ ◯ ◯ ◯ ◯ ◯ ◯

_____ ◯ ◯ ◯ ◯ ◯ ◯ ◯

_____ ◯ ◯ ◯ ◯ ◯ ◯ ◯

_____ ◯ ◯ ◯ ◯ ◯ ◯ ◯

_____ ◯ ◯ ◯ ◯ ◯ ◯ ◯

_____ ◯ ◯ ◯ ◯ ◯ ◯ ◯

_____ ◯ ◯ ◯ ◯ ◯ ◯ ◯

NOTE:

My Weekly Planner

DATE:

MOON PHASE: NEW MOON / WAXING / FULL MOON / WANING

FOCUS: REST. REFLECT. SET INTENTION / PLAN. INITIATE. ACTION
CONNECT. BE SEEN. RELEASE / COMPLETE. DELIVER. LET GO

TOP 3 PRIORITIES: **REMINDER:**

TO-DO LIST:

Weekly Schedule

Appointments / Workout / Meals

Date:

Monday

Tuesday

Wednesday

Thursday

Friday

Saturday

Sunday

Note

Weekly Check-In

DATE:

MOON PHASE:

CYCLE: Menstrual / Follicular / Ovulation / Luteal

MOOD:

BODY
How's your energy this week?

MIND
What is on your mind?

SPIRIT
How are you feeling?

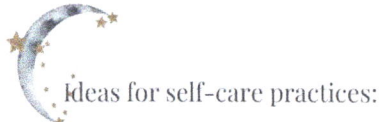

Ideas for self-care practices:

Habit Tracker

KEY FOCUS FOR THIS WEEK:

MY GOOD HABITS   M   T   W   TH   F   S   S

_____ ◯ ◯ ◯ ◯ ◯ ◯ ◯

_____ ◯ ◯ ◯ ◯ ◯ ◯ ◯

_____ ◯ ◯ ◯ ◯ ◯ ◯ ◯

_____ ◯ ◯ ◯ ◯ ◯ ◯ ◯

_____ ◯ ◯ ◯ ◯ ◯ ◯ ◯

_____ ◯ ◯ ◯ ◯ ◯ ◯ ◯

_____ ◯ ◯ ◯ ◯ ◯ ◯ ◯

_____ ◯ ◯ ◯ ◯ ◯ ◯ ◯

NOTE:

My Weekly Planner

DATE:

MOON PHASE: NEW MOON / WAXING / FULL MOON / WANING

FOCUS: REST. REFLECT. SET INTENTION / PLAN. INITIATE. ACTION
CONNECT. BE SEEN. RELEASE / COMPLETE. DELIVER. LET GO

TOP 3 PRIORITIES: **REMINDER:**

TO-DO LIST:

Weekly Schedule

Appointments / Workout / Meals

Date:

Monday

Tuesday

Wednesday

Thursday

Friday

Saturday

Sunday

Note

Weekly Check-In

DATE:

MOON PHASE:

CYCLE: Menstrual / Follicular / Ovulation / Luteal

MOOD:

BODY
How's your energy this week?

MIND
What is on your mind?

SPIRIT
How are you feeling?

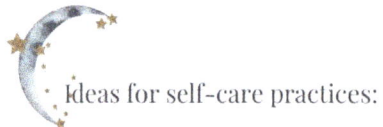
Ideas for self-care practices:

KEY FOCUS FOR THIS WEEK:

MY GOOD HABITS   M   T   W   TH   F   S   S

NOTE:

New Year Wish List

About Sze Wing Vetault

Sze Wing is a coach, author and creative entrepreneur. She works with career women, busy mums and purpose-driven business owners to become goddesses in all aspects of their lives. In other words, she helps them to uncover their feminine wisdom to find better work-life balance, more joy & vitality and sustainable success in life.

With a background in Economics (BSc.) and Political Sciences (MSc.), she has built a diverse career as a business consultant for government agencies, education enterprise and film & television companies.

Sze Wing speaks, writes and promotes in the health and wellness industry. She works with other authors to publish their non-fiction books and launch creative projects. She runs a blog & podcast and she is also a mum to two beautiful young children.

She loves to do yoga, dance and travel with her family. Her favourite morning ritual includes mediation, journaling and sipping a good cup of tea!

For more information, please visit her website at
www.SzeWingVetault.com

www.ingramcontent.com/pod-product-compliance
Lightning Source LLC
Chambersburg PA
CBHW051535010526
44107CB00064B/2734